Read & Respond

FOR KS2

PAGE 1

Read & Respond

FOR KS2

Author: Nikki Gamble

Development Editor: Rachel Mackinnon

Editor: Sarah Sodhi

Assistant Editor: Louise Titley

Series Designer: Anna Oliwa

Designer: Liz Gilbert

Illustrations: Anthony Browne
Ellen Hopkins, Beehive Illustrations

Text © 2009, Nikki Gamble © 2009 Scholastic Ltd

Designed using Adobe InDesign

Published by Scholastic Ltd, Villiers House,
Clarendon Avenue, Leamington Spa,
Warwickshire CV32 5PR
www.scholastic.co.uk

Printed by Bell & Bain
1 2 3 4 5 6 7 8 9   9 0 1 2 3 4 5 6 7 8

British Library Cataloguing-in-Publication Data
A catalogue record for this book is available from
the British Library.

ISBN 978-1407-11397-5

Acknowledgements

The publishers gratefully acknowledge permission to reproduce the following copyright material: **Walker Books** for the use of text and illustrations from *Gorilla* by Anthony Browne © 1983, Anthony Browne (1983, Julia MacRae Books). Every effort has been made to trace copyright holders for the works reproduced in this book, and the publishers apologise for any inadvertent omissions.

Gorilla

About the book

First published in 1983, *Gorilla* is one of Anthony Browne's most well-loved picture books with a broad appeal to readers of all ages. It was awarded the Kate Greenaway Medal for illustration, selected as one of the top ten picture books of the Carnegie and Greenaway Medals, and awarded the Kurt Maschler Award for the integration of text and image.

Hannah loves gorillas, but she has never seen one. Her father is too busy to take her to the zoo, but when her birthday arrives he buys her a toy gorilla. Disappointed, Hannah throws the gorilla into a corner. Then, magically, the gorilla transforms into a real gorilla, puts on her father's hat and coat and takes Hannah on an adventure to the zoo. Waking the next day, she rushes downstairs, eager to tell her father about her night-time adventure. The story ends happily with father and daughter, hand in hand, on the way to the zoo.

Browne's books often feature a solitary or lonely child. The story is a child's personal journey, transformation and the promise of happiness. Gorilla characters often appear in Browne's stories. He says, 'I am fascinated by them and the contrast they represent – their huge strength and gentleness.'

Gorilla's multiple levels of meaning make it a text that can be shared with children of different ages and abilities. It is a picture book that can be appreciated by children in KS2. The plot is straightforward, the text is simple and the narrative is direct. By contrast, the pictures are detailed and demand close reading. Watercolour images blend realism and surrealism, creating an everyday world that exists simultaneously with a landscape of the imagination. In the interaction between text and images, the meanings of the book can be discovered.

Gorilla is set in the home and so can be included in a literacy unit featuring stories in familiar settings. Family is a recurring theme in Anthony Browne's books, making them a rich resource for study of stories by the same author. In *Gorilla*, a visit to the zoo is a birthday treat, although there are hints that this is not the happiest experience for the captive animals. This presents excellent cross-curricular opportunities for studying humans' relationships with animals and the natural world in Citizenship/PSHE. This theme recurs in his later books, *Zoo* and *Little Beauty*.

About the author

Anthony Browne is an internationally recognised author and illustrator. In 2000, he was awarded the Hans Christian Medal for illustration and nominated Children's Laureate 2009–2011. As a young boy he wanted to be a cartoonist, journalist or a boxer. After leaving school he attended Leeds Art College and graduated in 1967 with a graphic arts degree. He worked as a medical illustrator and then a designer for greetings cards before becoming a full-time writer and illustrator of children's books.

Facts and figures
Gorilla
First published in 1983.
Winner of the Kate Greenaway Medal and Kurt Maschler Award.
Anthony Browne talks about his work on the DVD *Through Gorilla's Eyes*, available from Children's Authors TV.

Guided reading

Managing the guided reading sessions

Gorilla is a multilayered picture book, which is well suited to guided and group reading. It is essential that children have opportunities to experience the pictures and develop personal responses independently. Guided prompts should open up possibilities for interpretation rather than simply requiring 'correct' answers or privileging the teacher's interpretation over the children's. The following sequence is intended to give children space to develop their own thinking, which can then be developed through group interaction.

During teacher-led guided reading sessions use a range of questions and prompts and strategies for developing group discussion. Productive questions will allow you to elicit personal responses and relate the text to the children's experiences, as well as probe the themes, predict, reflect, speculate and evaluate. Encourage the children to respond to each other directly (rather than through the teacher) and to ask each other questions.

First reading

Introduce the book and invite the children to talk briefly about any books by Anthony Browne that they have already read. Give each child a copy of the book and allow them five to ten minutes to read the book at their own pace. Expressly ask them not to discuss it with anyone else at this stage. This is to allow individuals an opportunity to develop their own ideas without being influenced by others.

Read the book aloud to the group at an unhurried natural reading pace. For less confident readers this stage of the process provides a good model of 'how the story goes'. More confident readers can share the reading. At this stage, do not disrupt the flow by stopping to ask probing questions. Allow a short time for reflection before you turn the page.

Give each child a sheet of A3 paper divided into quadrants with a copy of the jacket cover stuck to the centre of the paper. At the top of each quadrant write one of these headings: 'The things I liked most about *Gorilla* were…'; 'This book reminded me of these things…'; 'I was puzzled by…'; and 'The questions I would like to ask Anthony Browne are…'. Give one or two examples for each of the headings. For instance, the book might remind them of a personal experience, such as receiving a disappointing birthday present, or it might remind them of another book they have read.

Ask them to re-read the book independently and then jot down some ideas on their large sheets of paper. Stress that there are no right or wrong answers, and that they can write or draw their ideas. Allow about ten minutes for this activity. These notes will help them to remember what they are thinking. Committing thinking to paper, in whatever form, means the children will begin to have some commitment to their ideas and be less likely to be swayed by the interpretations of the dominant members of the group.

Gather the group together and invite each child to share their ideas about the book, using the large sheets of paper to aid the feedback. Encourage the group to listen attentively, without interruption or comment. Explain that there will be time for discussion later. At this stage it is important that every child's ideas are given equal consideration. Emphasise listening skills and the value of learning from others who may have different ideas. Alternatively, ask the children to share their ideas in pairs, emphasising that they should listen to each other without interruption. After listening to the initial responses, invite their comments by asking: *Did someone have an idea different to yours? How did it make you think differently about this book?*

Page by page

Revisit the text encouraging deeper reflection. Explain that you are going to read the book page by page and that the children can talk about whatever interests them. Encourage them to think about the puzzles and questions that they have noted on their sheets of paper.

Guided reading

At breakfast

Read the page starting *Hannah loved gorillas.* Ask: *What sort of child do you think Hannah is? Why do you think that?* Look at the facing page and encourage the children to think about the characters and how they relate to each other. Ask: *What does this picture make you feel? What do you imagine Hannah and Hannah's father are feeling?* Point out that we can't see Hannah's expression, so we have to use other clues. Ask: *What reasons could there be that Hannah's father is too busy to go to the zoo? Do you notice anything about the colours and shapes Anthony Browne has used to paint this picture?*

Busy working

Read the next page, starting *He went to work every day,* and look at the picture on the facing page. Ask the children what questions they think Hannah asks her father. Discuss his responses and invite them to consider whether parents should always stop what they are doing to listen to their children. Encourage an exchange of different points of view.

Hannah alone

Read the next page, starting *But the next day.* Guide the children to look closely at the large image. Ask the children to describe what they see here. What can they see in the shadows and what do they see in the light. Invite them to consider why Anthony Browne might have made the picture like this.

In bed

Read the following page, starting *The night before her birthday.* After the children have discussed what interests them in the pictures, ask them how they can tell what Hannah is feeling. What do they notice about the way the bed has been drawn? Encourage them to relate Hannah's feelings to their own experiences. Have they ever felt disappointment with a present?

Ask the children to summarise what they have learned about Hannah, her father and their relationship.

The gorilla

Read the page beginning *Hannah threw the gorilla.* Ask: *What is the* amazing *thing that happens on these pages? How would you feel if you saw this gorilla at the foot of your bed?* Turn back to the previous page and compare the way that Anthony Browne has drawn these pictures. For example, draw their attention to the size of the bedstead and reflect on how this affects the reader's understanding of what is happening in the story.

Trip to the zoo

Read the next eight pages, starting *Hannah was frightened* and ending *She thought they were beautiful. But sad.* Divide into three parts (gorilla, Hannah and the narrator) and choose children to read these parts (two groups of three if working in a group with six children).

Remind the children to read expressively, prompting them with questions such as: *What tone of voice would the gorilla use if he wanted to reassure Hannah?* Invite the children to talk about what interests them in these pages.

Gather the group together and discuss how the animals have been drawn. Ask: *What are they looking at? Do you think the animals are aware that they are caged? What makes you think that?*

Night-time adventures

Read the next six pages, up to *Hannah had never been so happy.* Encourage the children to notice details in the pictures by asking questions, such as: *Can you see Hannah and the gorilla watching the film?*

Compare the café scene with the earlier kitchen scene. Invite the children to work in pairs to identify the similarities and differences between these two pictures. For instance, both pictures show Hannah facing dad/gorilla across the table.

However, the colours are warmer, Hannah seems to be closer to the gorilla, and there is an abundance of food. Ask: *What does the second picture make you feel? What do you think Hannah is feeling at this point in the story?*

Look at the picture of Hannah and the gorilla dancing on the lawn. Ask: *In what way is their dancing different to the gorilla couples?* (Hannah's feet are placed over the gorilla's, playing a game like father and daughter.)

A Happy Birthday

Read to the end of the story. Discuss the children's responses to this section with prompts, such as: *What do you think Hannah dreamed about that night? Apart from the word* rushed *in the text, how can we tell that Hannah came downstairs in a hurry? What do you think Hannah is thinking when the text reads* Hannah looked at him?

Allow two minutes for the children to scan the story from the beginning, refreshing their memory of what happens, and then invite them to consider what changes have taken place.

Ask them to express what the story is about in their own words. Some children will respond at plot level, while others might start to express their ideas thematically. Make this explicit in your responses, for example, *That's interesting Jack. You haven't told us what happens in the story, you've told us what you think the story means.*

Shared reading

Extract 1

● In pairs, ask the children to talk about what we learn about Hannah at the beginning of the story. Extend the children's thinking with prompts, such as: *Do you think she likes being alone? Why do you think she likes gorillas so much?*

● Tell them that Anthony Browne is also fascinated by gorillas because of they are strong yet gentle. Ask: *How many times are gorillas mentioned in this passage? Why do you think Anthony Browne repeats the same word so many times?* (It emphasises how obsessed Hannah is.)

● Relate this passage to the children's experiences. Do they have an interest that they feel passionate about? Ask: *Why do you think Hannah's father is too busy?*

● Move from the specific to the general, asking: *When do parents usually say they are too busy?* Challenge them to think about this from different viewpoints. Ask: *Should parents always stop what they are doing to listen to their children?* Allow for free-flowing discussion rather than seeking a 'yes' or 'no' answer to this question.

Extract 2

● Read the extract and then ask: *Why does Hannah go to bed* tingling with excitement? Although the passage says that Hannah has asked for a gorilla, the children have to infer that it is the expectation of receiving one that causes the excitement. Point out that Anthony Browne does not actually say this but we have to think about what it means.

● Read the last sentence and ask why the word *was* is italicised.

● Ask the children to work in pairs, practising reading this with appropriate expression.

● Delete the word *just* from this sentence and re-read it. Encourage the children to think about how this affects our response to the passage. Make the point that every word counts and that even small, ordinary words can make a difference to a story.

● Highlight the phrase *tingling with excitement*. In pairs, ask the children to come up with some other phrases to convey Hannah's excitement. Share and evaluate these ideas.

Extract 3

● Read the passage and draw the children's attention to the direct speech. Explain that these were the words that are actually spoken by Hannah and the gorilla.

● Ask for a volunteer to highlight all the words spoken by the gorilla and another volunteer to highlight all the words spoken by Hannah.

● Point out the punctuation used and explain that this helps us know how to read the passage.

● In groups of three, ask the children to re-read the passage, taking the roles of Hannah, the gorilla and the narrator.

● Look at the picture. Ask: *What do you think Hannah is thinking? How can we tell that she is not afraid of the gorilla?* (Her body language, their eye contact, the happy face on the light switch.)

Extract 1

Hannah loved gorillas. She read books about gorillas, she watched gorillas on television, and she drew pictures of gorillas. But she had never seen a real gorilla.

Her father didn't have time to take her to see one at the zoo. He didn't have time for anything.

Text and illustration © 1983, Anthony Browne.

Extract 2

The night before her birthday, Hannah went to bed tingling with excitement – she had asked her father for a gorilla!

In the middle of the night, Hannah woke up and saw a very small parcel at the foot of the bed. It *was* a gorilla, but it was just a toy.

Text and illustration © 1983, Anthony Browne.

Extract 3

Hannah was frightened. "Don't be frightened, Hannah," said the gorilla, "I won't hurt you. I just wondered if you'd like to go to the zoo."

The gorilla had such a nice smile that Hannah wasn't afraid. "I'd love to," she said.

They both crept downstairs, and Hannah put on her coat. The gorilla put on her father's hat and coat. "A perfect fit," he whispered.

Text and illustration © 1983, Anthony Browne.

Plot, character and setting

Hannah alone

> **Objective:** To infer character's feelings in fiction.
> **What you need:** Copies of *Gorilla* or an enlarged copy of the illustration showing Hannah in the corner of the room watching television, A3 copy of photocopiable page 15.
> **Cross-curricular links:** PSHE, art and design.

What to do

● Before reading the book, invite the children to develop a profile of Hannah using visual clues.
● In pairs, ask the children to discuss their initial impressions of Hannah and feed back to the class.
● Extend the children's thinking by asking questions, such as: *What do you notice about the wallpaper in this room? Why do you think Anthony Browne has drawn it like this? What impression is created by the girl sitting on the floor in the corner? Would it be different if she were sitting on a comfortable armchair?*

● In pairs, ask the children to write down any questions they would like to ask Hannah. As a class, share the questions and speculate about the answers. Explain that this is exploratory and that they will find out more when they read the book.
● Ask: *What do you think this girl dreams about?*
● Distribute copies of the photocopiable sheet and invite the children to add notes in each of the circles.
● Gather the class to review their ideas.

> **Differentiation**
> **For older/more confident learners:** Challenge the children to infer thoughts, feelings, wishes and dreams.
> **For younger/less confident learners:** Support the children to describe what they see in the pictures.

It reminded me of…

> **Objective:** To interrogate texts to deepen and clarify understanding and response.
> **What you need:** Copies of *Gorilla*, photocopiable page 16.
> **Cross-curricular links:** PSHE, history.

What to do

● When the children are familiar with the story, work on the reading strategy 'making connections'. They should relate what they read to what they already know, to make better sense of the story.
● Explain that when you read *Gorilla* everyone in the class will have different thoughts because of our different experiences. Model this by selecting part of the story and saying, for example: *This part of the story reminds me of a time that I really wanted a puppy, but my parents wouldn't let me*

have one because we lived in a flat where pets were not allowed. Write your connection on a sticky note and stick it in the book
● Distribute the photocopiable sheet. Explain to the children that they can choose any part of the story that reminded them of something, and draw this in the left-hand box. In the box on the right-hand side of the page, let them write about the memory that was sparked by the story.

> **Differentiation**
> **For older/more confident learners:** Challenge children to write an entry in their reading journals, describing the connections that occurred to them while they were reading the story.
> **For younger/less confident learners:** Support children with further discussion with an adult in a guided group.

Plot, character and setting

Think about it!

Objective: To deduce characters' reasons for behaviour from their actions.
What you need: Enlarged copy of the illustration depicting Hannah in her father's study, A1 sheet of paper.
Cross-curricular link: Art and design.

What to do

● Guide the children to look closely at Anthony Browne's illustrations, considering the significance of small details and using visual clues to infer inner thoughts.
● Invite an open response to the illustration by asking: *What do you see?* Prompt the children to consider how the details evoke specific responses in the reader. Use prompts, such as: *Why do you think Hannah is so far away from her father? Is he aware she is behind him? Does he look relaxed? What do you notice about the photograph on the*
desktop? Do the straight lines of the chair back remind you of anything? Have you seen this pattern elsewhere in the book? What do you notice about the colours? Why does Hannah have her hands behind her back?
● In pairs, ask the children to write down what they think Hannah is thinking. Write their ideas in large thought bubbles on the A1 sheet of paper. Do the same for Hannah's father.
● Make the point that people sometimes say and think different things. Relate this idea to the children's own experiences.

Differentiation
For older/more confident learners: Challenge the children to articulate the possible differences between the characters' thoughts and what they say.
For younger/less confident learners: Undertake a 'hot-seating' session with the children before noting the characters' thoughts.

Colour it red, colour it blue

Objective: To explore the way setting evokes mood and atmosphere.
What you need: Copies of breakfast scene (A) and café scene (B) illustrations, dictionaries, photocopiable page 17, sticky notes.
Cross-curricular link: Art and design.

What to do

● This activity explores how setting and mood are communicated through colour, shape, composition and body language.
● Organise the children into small groups. Distribute copies of the illustrations (half the class has illustration A and half has illustration B) and the photocopiable sheet.
● Ask the children to select words they think describe their scene. Encourage them to use dictionaries to check definitions.
● Look at illustration A together. Invite volunteers to add words that best describe the
scene to the illustration using sticky notes. Ask: *What would you see/hear/feel if you were Hannah?*
● Encourage the children to look closely at the details. Ask questions, such as: *How are Hannah and her father seated? Where are they looking? Would the scene feel different if the kitchen was painted yellow? What shapes and patterns do you notice in this picture?*
● Repeat the process for illustration B.
● Compare the two scenes. Ask: *How are they similar/different?* Ask the children to draw a happy and a sad version of the same scene.

Differentiation
For older/more confident learners: Challenge children to extend the list of words using a thesaurus. Encourage them to be exact and give full explanations of their selection.
For younger/less confident learners: Select words that are most appropriate to the children's abilities.

Plot, character and setting

Transformation

> **Objective:** To understand that in narrative texts time can be communicated through a sequence of visual frames.
> **What you need:** Copies of the double-page spread showing the gorilla's transformation, percussion instruments (wood blocks, triangles and guiros), large sheets of paper folded into four squares.
> **Cross-curricular link:** Art and design.

What to do

● This activity looks at how a transformation can be depicted by using a sequence of frames.
● Read the double-page spread together. Then ask the children if they know any stories where toys or characters transform from one thing into another.
● Let the children read the text in pairs and then tell the story of what is happening in the pictures.

● Gather the class together and demonstrate how percussion instruments can be used to signal each stage in the transformation.
● Invite the children to enact this part of the story. One child reads the text and then strikes the percussion instrument four times while the other child mimes the transformation.
● Encourage the children to draw their own transformation scenes based on a favourite toy or everyday object.

> **Differentiation**
> **For older/more confident learners:** Challenge the children to create a transformation scene in which one object slowly turns into another, such as a kettle into a cat. Use Anthony Browne's book *Changes* as a source of ideas.
> **For younger/less confident learners:** Let the children sequence a ready-made series of images before working with a partner to create their own.

A magical adventure

> **Objective:** To develop empathy with characters.
> **What you need:** Copies of illustrations of Hannah and the gorilla (visit to the zoo; cinema; café; dancing on the lawn), paper, pencils, digital camera.
> **Cross-curricular link:** ICT.

What to do

● Organise the children in small groups. Distribute the copies of different illustrations to each group.
● Invite the groups to create a freeze-frame to represent their scene. Challenge them to think about body language, position and eye contact.
● View the still images and take digital photographs.
● Distribute paper and pencils. Ask the children to imagine that they are Hannah. Invite them

to close their eyes as you recount the magical adventure in your own words. For example, *The night was clear, bright and silent, nothing was stirring except the neighbour's cat on her late-night prowl. Gorilla took you by the hand and soon you were swinging through the trees, across the night sky to the zoo.*
● Invite the children to write or draw their favourite memory of the adventure.
● Display the images with the memories, or scan them to create a slideshow presentation.

> **Differentiation**
> **For older/more confident learners:** Challenge the children to create a short storyboard of still images.
> **For younger/less confident learners:** Support the children to explore the effect of different positions for their still image, before choosing a final one.

Plot, character and setting

Before and after

> **Objective:** To develop knowledge of stories that use transformation as a plot device.
> **What you need:** Copies of *Gorilla*, photocopiable page 18.

What to do

● This activity is designed to help the children identify a pivotal event in the story. In this instance, they will look at the transformation of the toy gorilla.

● Re-read the story together. Ask: *What happens in the story that changes things for Hannah?* (Her encounter with the gorilla.)

● Ask the children to work in groups of four to create two freeze-frame images: one depicting Hannah and her father before Hannah's adventures with the gorilla; and the second showing Hannah and her father after the night-time adventure.

● Gather the class together and share the freeze-frames. Evaluate the children's use of body language, gesture and gaze. Invite the children to suggest words to describe each of the freeze-frames.

● Distribute copies of the photocopiable sheet and invite the children to draw two pictures to show how things change after the gorilla's visit.

> **Differentiation**
> **For older/more confident learners:** Challenge the children to identify the pivotal moment in other picture books where a change is brought about by a significant event. Useful books include *Where the Wild Things Are* by Maurice Sendak, *The Tunnel* by Anthony Browne, *Beegu* by Alexis Deacon, and *The Bear Under the Stairs* by Helen Cooper.
> **For younger/less confident learners:** Organise the children to work in mixed-ability groups, so less confident children can gain support from others in the group.

Soundtrack

> **Objective:** To use sound-tracking as a strategy for interrogating text and deepening response.
> **What you need:** Copies of *Gorilla*, copies of relevant illustrations from *Gorilla*.
> **Cross-curricular link:** Music.

What to do

● Invite the children to make music to represent the different moods in the story so that each section becomes a musical movement. Use this as a soundtrack to a slideshow of images.

● With the children, agree a sequence of key events, such as: Hannah alone, gorilla's transformation, the zoo, the cinema, the café, dancing on the lawn, Hannah opens her birthday cards. List these on a large sheet of paper. Select an illustration to accompany each event.

● Seat the children in a circle. Focus on one event, such as the cinema, and discuss sounds that might be heard (film music, sound effects, rustling of popcorn, voices whispering). Prompt them to think beyond the obvious.

● Let the children choose an appropriate sound using their voices (words and non-verbal sounds), bodies and percussive materials. Let them demonstrate sounds around the circle. If sounds are too similar give them thinking time to suggest another.

● Organise the children in groups. Give each group an illustration to create a soundtrack for.

● Gather the class together and read the story adding the soundtrack.

> **Differentiation**
> **For older/more confident learners:** Challenge children with greater musical experience to compose and notate a short piece of music.
> **For younger/less confident learners:** Organise the children to work in mixed-ability groups, so less confident children can gain support from others in the group.

Hannah alone

● Look at the pictures of Hannah in the first part of the story. Discuss with a partner what sort of character you think Hannah is. Write down your ideas in the circles below.

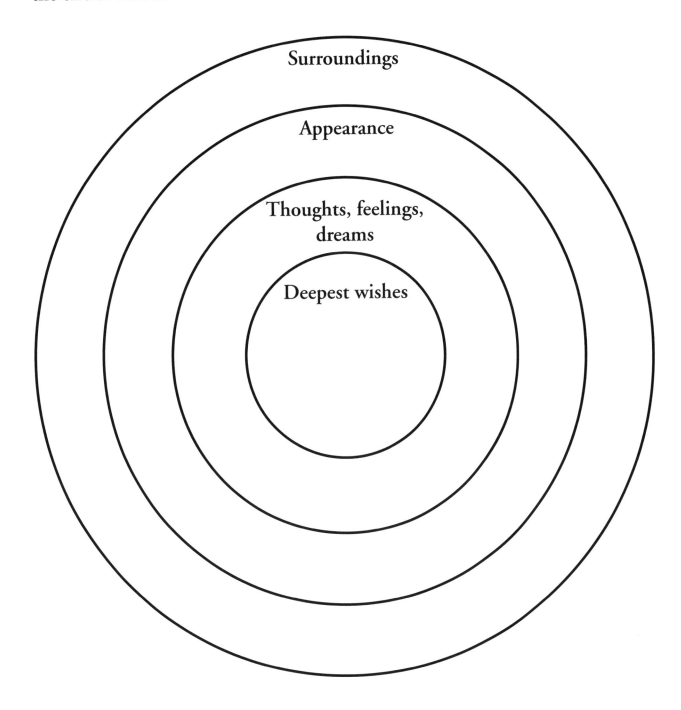

Surroundings

Appearance

Thoughts, feelings, dreams

Deepest wishes

It reminded me of...

- Everyone will have different thoughts when reading a book because it will remind them of their different experiences. Choose any part of the story that reminds you of something. Draw the part of the story in the left-hand box, and write about what it reminds you of in the right-hand box.

Reminded me of...

This part of the story...

Colour it red, colour it blue

● Look at these words. Choose those that best describe the illustration you have been given from *Gorilla*. Use a dictionary to check the definitions if you need to.

cold	warm	friendly
unfriendly	silent	conversation
depressed	happy	fun
contented	bleak	cheerful
genial	sociable	close
distant	miserable	friends
dreary	dismal	feast
bright	drab	lonely

Before and after

- The arrival of the gorilla seems to change things for Hannah. Draw two pictures, one showing how things were for Hannah before the gorilla arrived in the left-hand box, and one showing how they were afterwards, in the right-hand box.

After

Before

Illustration © Ellen Hopkins, Beehive Illustrations.

Talk about it

Asking questions

> **Objective:** To generate questions and initiate dialogue.
> **What you need:** Copies of *Gorilla*, large sheets of paper, coloured highlighters.

What to do

● Carry out this activity after the first reading of the book.

● After reading, invite the children to think of questions they want to ask about the story.

● List all of their questions without comment so that the children implicitly understand that all questions are equally valid. For example: *Why is the coat a perfect fit for the gorilla? Why is Hannah's dad always busy? Why are there two handles on the front door?* If all the questions are listed, there is likely to be a wide range. Some will be open and others will be closed questions.

● Review the questions with the class and group them using coloured highlighters. For example, blue for questions about Hannah's relationship with her father, green for questions about zoos, and so on.

● Ask the children to select the group of questions that interests them the most and use these as the basis for discussion. Use dialogic techniques to promote the discussion, such as extended exchanges that help clarify and promote thinking, argumentation to challenge children's opinions and seek justification, and so on.

> **Differentiation**
> **For older/more confident learners:** Ask specific children more challenging questions about the text.
> **For younger/less confident learners:** Ask specific children less challenging questions about the text.

Alone or lonely?

> **Objective:** To express feelings and to listen attentively to others.
> **What you need:** Copy of the illustration showing Hannah alone in the corner of her room.
> **Cross-curricular link:** PSHE.

What to do

● Organise the children into a sharing circle.

● Show the children the picture of Hannah sitting alone in her room. Ask: *What do you think Hannah is feeling? How do you know that?*

● Explain that the subject for the sharing circle is, 'I remember a time when I felt lonely'. Ask: *Can you remember a time when you were alone?* Maybe a close friend had left the school, or everyone at home was too busy to play with you. Give the children a minute to recall their memories.

● Work around the circle asking children to share their memories if they want to.

● Talk about what lessons, if any, can we learn from being lonely (empathising with others, finding things to keep occupied, approaching friends, and so on).

● Ask: *Is being alone the same as being lonely? Do you ever enjoy being alone? Next time you are lonely, is there anything you can do to help yourself?*

● Take on the role of Hannah's father. Invite the children to give you advice on how you could communicate better with Hannah.

> **Differentiation**
> **For older/more confident learners:** Challenge the children to listen to a partner's experiences before writing a simple recount.
> **For younger/less confident learners:** Support the children to sketch their ideas before speaking.

Talk about it

Should zoos be banned?

> **Objective:** To understand different ways to take the lead and support others in groups.
>
> **What you need:** Copies of the two double-page spreads that show Hannah at the zoo, photocopiable page 22, large sheet of paper for each group with the discussion topic at the top and two columns labelled 'No, because…' and 'Yes, because…'.

What to do

● Re-read the pages about Hannah's visit to the zoo. Organise the children in groups of four, distribute the photocopiable sheet and assign each member of the group a different discussion role.

● Introduce the discussion topic, 'Should zoos be banned?'

● Ask the groups to discuss the topic, letting the note maker record their ideas on their sheet.

● Gather the class and ask each reporter to feed back on the discussion.

● Summarise the main points and extend children's thinking using dialogic techniques. Model language, such as *I don't agree with… because…*

● After further discussion, take a vote on whether zoos should be banned.

● Ask the observers who spoke well in each group. What could the groups do better next time?

● Follow up by reading Anthony Browne's *Zoo*. Ask: *Do you think Anthony Browne likes zoos?*

> **Differentiation**
>
> **For older/more confident learners:** The children will not need to be assigned discussion roles if they have experience of self-managed discussion.
>
> **For younger/less confident learners:** Let the children use prompt cards to aid the discussion.

Chat show

> **Objective:** To respond appropriately to the contributions of others in the light of alternative viewpoints.
>
> **What you need:** Copies of *Gorilla*.

What to do

● Talk about what a chat show is and view a short extract if possible.

● Explain that the class will be exploring the story from three different points of view, by improvising a chat show.

● Briefly revise different types of questions highlighting the differences between open and closed questions.

● In groups of four, ask the children to write a list of questions that they would like to ask each character. For example, they might ask Hannah's father: *Why were you always so busy when Hannah wanted you to take her to the zoo?* They might ask the gorilla: *What made you visit Hannah on the night before her birthday?*

● Let the children improvise a chat show, playing the following roles: TV presenter, Gorilla, Hannah, Hannah's father.

● Gather the class, view one or two of the improvisations and discuss any issues that arise.

● As a final reflection, ask: *How did the drama aid our understanding of the characters in this story?*

> **Differentiation**
>
> **For older/more confident learners:** Organise the children to work in mixed-ability groups, so more confident children can give support to others in the group.
>
> **For younger/less confident learners:** Organise the children to work in mixed-ability groups, so less confident children can gain support from others in the group.

Talk about it

Talking about the story

Objective: To understand and use a variety of ways to criticise constructively and respond to criticism.
What you need: Copies of *Gorilla*, photocopiable page 23.

What to do

● Explain that readers are likely to have different ideas about *Gorilla*. When we talk about a book we can learn from other people's ideas and they can learn from us.
● Remind the children about the characteristics of good group talk: listening thoughtfully to others; explaining ideas; disagreeing respectfully.
● Read the statements aloud from the photocopiable sheet and check the children's understanding. Explain that you want the children to talk about their ideas. There are no right or wrong answers, but they need to justify their thinking. For example: *I think Hannah's mother lives somewhere else because she isn't mentioned in the story.* Highlight the words *I think* and *because*.
● Make explicit other language skills, such as supporting each other's thinking or expressing an alternative point of view.
● Organise the children into groups to discuss the statements.
● Gather the class and share their ideas.

Differentiation
For older/more confident learners: Adapt the statements to provide greater challenge for the children. For example, *The story is told from Hannah's point of view* or *The story in words and in pictures have different points of view.*
For younger/less confident learners: Select statements that challenge the children at an appropriate level. For example, *The chimpanzee feels safe in the zoo* or *The orang-utan is unhappy in the zoo.* Reinforce the difference between argumentation and disputational talk.

Puppet show

Objective: To perform a scripted scene making use of dramatic conventions.
What you need: Copies of *Gorilla*, photocopiable page 24, materials for making puppets.

What to do

● Explain that the class is going to make a puppet theatre and devise a puppet show of *Gorilla*.
● In small groups, let the children improvise the conversation between Hannah and her father at the breakfast table.
● Revise the conventions of script writing and demonstrate how to create a script from the book by modelling the beginning of the story. Ask the children what was said in their improvisations and use this to script the drama.
● Allocate each group a different part of the story to improvise.
● Gather the class and share the improvisations. Ask the groups to script their part of the play, before assembling the whole script and making copies for the children.
● Make wooden-spoon puppets and scenery for the puppet theatre.
● Rehearse and refine the play before performing to a younger class, parents or at assembly. Invite constructive feedback from the audience.

Differentiation
For older/more confident learners: Challenge the children to extend the script, deciding what happens next.
For younger/less confident learners: Let the children create a storyboard and use this as a prop to aid storytelling with puppets.

Should zoos be banned?

● Read the tasks for your role in the discussion. Make sure you complete all your tasks.

Chair

● Make sure everyone understands the task.

● Make sure you have enough time to discuss everything.

● Summarise the group's ideas.

Observer

● Does everyone have a turn?

● Do people speak clearly?

● Do group members listen to each other?

● Do they ask each other questions?

Note maker

● Write down the main points.

● If you miss an idea say, "Can you repeat that?" or "Can you say that more slowly?"

Reporter

● Agree the main points to feed back to the class.

● Represent everyone's ideas.

● Speak confidently and clearly when feeding back to the class.

Illustrations © Ellen Hopkins, Beehive Illustrations.

Talk about it

Talking about the story

● Talk together to decide if you agree, disagree or are unsure about these statements.

1. Hannah's mother doesn't live with Hannah and her father.

2. Hannah's mother died when Hannah was younger.

3. Hannah prefers spending time with the gorilla to spending time with her father.

4. Hannah's father works hard because he wants to make a good life for Hannah.

5. Hannah's father enjoys work more than he enjoys spending time with Hannah.

6. Hannah is bored.

7. Hannah is an imaginative girl.

8. Hannah likes gorillas because they remind her of her father.

9. The gorillas in the zoo are pleased to see Hannah and the gorilla.

10. The gorilla appears because Hannah has wished so hard for him.

11. The gorilla just exists in Hannah's imagination.

12. This is a magical story and the gorilla appears by magic.

● Write two statements about Anthony Browne's *Gorilla*.

_____

_____

_____

_____

Puppet show

What you need

Wooden spoon
Scrap material (wool, buttons, fake fur)
Indelible marker pens or acrylic paint
Glue or masking tape
Thick pipe cleaners

What to do

● Choose one of the characters from the story.

1. Draw or paint a face on your wooden spoon. Hannah and her father could have a face drawn on each side of the spoon: a happy face and a sad face. 	**2.** Decorate the puppet with scraps of material. Copy the clothes that your character is wearing in the book. 
3. Create hair by gluing wool to the head. 	**4.** Tie pipe cleaners around the wooden spoon to form the arms and legs. 

Illustrations © Ellen Hopkins, Beehive Illustrations.

Get writing

Dear diary

> **Objective:** To write a diary entry using a diary format.
> **What you need:** Copies of *Gorilla*, display of books written in diary format such as *Dear Diary* by Sara Fanelli and *Dougal's Deep Sea Diary* by Simon Bartram (optional), photocopiable page 28.
> **Cross-curricular link:** PSHE.

What to do

● Ask the class: *Does anyone keep a diary? Why do people write in diaries?* Draw out the children's different ideas. Suggest that a lonely child like Hannah might find it comforting to write in a diary. Writing in a diary can be like sharing your feelings with a friend.

● Ask for a volunteer to be Hannah and use a hot-seating session to explore her thoughts and feelings at the beginning of the story.

● In pairs, ask the children to talk about the sorts of things Hannah might write in her diary. Suggest they re-read the pages up to *They never did anything together* and use these to generate ideas. Gather the class together and discuss their thoughts.

● Distribute copies of the photocopiable sheet and invite the children to write diary entries for Monday, Tuesday and Wednesday, using the prompts on the sheet.

> **Differentiation**
> **For older/more confident learners:** Challenge the children to write their diary entry without the writing prompts on the photocopiable sheet. Expect longer, more developed entries.
> **For younger/less confident learners:** Make sure the children benefit from the hot-seating session and paired discussion before writing their diary entries.

What happens next?

> **Objective:** To continue a story using the characters, setting and structure from a known story.
> **What you need:** Copies of *Gorilla*, blank books in landscape format with five spreads, drawing materials, A3 sheet of paper.
> **Cross-curricular link:** Art and design.

What to do

● This activity provides an opportunity for the children to use the structures of *Gorilla* to create a new picture book.

● Review the ending of the story together. Ask: *Do you like the ending? Do you have any questions about what might happen next?*

● Compare the illustration at the end of the story (Hannah holding her father's hand) with the illustration opposite the café scene. Suggest that the ending is really the beginning of a new

story: the adventures of Hannah and her father.

● In pairs, invite the children to list things that Hannah might do with her father. Gather the class and pool everyone's suggestions.

● Record the children's ideas on an A3 sheet of paper, labelled: Hannah's birthday morning; first adventure; second adventure; third adventure; return home.

● Invite the children to write and illustrate their own stories, design the front jacket and write a blurb and reviews for the back cover.

> **Differentiation**
> **For older/more confident learners:** Challenge the children to write and illustrate their story in the same style as Anthony Browne.
> **For younger/less confident learners:** Children work in a group to write different parts of the story for a group book. Give additional help in guided writing.

Get writing

Gorillas

> **Objective:** To research, plan and write a slideshow presentation about gorillas.
> **What you need:** Information about gorillas (online and books), interactive whiteboard, internet access, photocopiable page 29.
> **Cross-curricular link:** ICT.

What to do

● Tell the class that Anthony Browne likes gorillas because they can be strong and gentle at the same time. Ask: *Does the gorilla in his story have these characteristics?* Explain that you are going to find out about gorillas living in the wild to create a slideshow presentation.

● Draw a two-column table on the board. In the left column list the things that the children already know about gorillas. In the right column list the things that they would like to find out.

● Using an enlarged copy of the photocopiable sheet, show how the children's questions can be organised on the planner. For example, *Are gorillas vegetarians?* can fit in the section, 'What do gorillas eat?'.

● Discuss where the children can find answers to their questions. Revise how to locate information efficiently using retrieval devices.

● In pairs, ask the children to use the different sources to make notes about gorillas. They should write a few sentences to answer each question.

● Use the information to make a slideshow presentation. Answer one question on each slide.

> **Differentiation**
> **For older/more confident learners:** Challenge the children to show their presentations to another class, school or parents.
> **For younger/less confident learners:** Give the children a set of questions that can each be answered with a sentence.

Father's story

> **Objective:** To empathise with characters and tell a story from an alternative point of view.
> **What you need:** Copies of *Gorilla*.

What to do

● *Gorilla* is told essentially from Hannah's viewpoint. This activity gives the children the opportunity to explore events from a different perspective.

● Discuss the children's responses to Hannah's father, both at the beginning and the end of the story. Ask: *Does Hannah's father change?*

● Compare the illustration showing Hannah at breakfast with the illustration of her opening her birthday cards. Ask the children to describe the body language in both pictures.

● Prompt the children to consider possible reasons for Hannah's father's behaviour. Probe the children's responses, for example, ask: *Why do you think Hannah's father works so hard?*

● In pairs, ask the children to improvise a conversation between Hannah and her father at the breakfast table. Gather the class and view one of the improvisations. Use 'thought tracking' to uncover Hannah's father's thoughts and feelings. Repeat the process for an event at the end of the story.

● In role as Hannah's father, invite the children to write a letter to Hannah explaining why he has been so busy.

> **Differentiation**
> **For older/more confident learners:** Challenge the children to explore Hannah's father's thoughts and feelings using dramatic monologue instead of thought tracking. Freeze the improvisation and let the father speak his inner thoughts to an audience.
> **For younger/less confident learners:** Let the children take photographs at various points in their improvisation. Construct a photo story with speech bubbles for Hannah's father's thoughts.

Get writing

Make a map

Objective: To refine a response to setting and understand how setting relates to the story action.
What you need: Large sheets of paper, drawing materials.
Cross-curricular link: Art and design.

What to do

● This activity helps the children to chart the journey in the story by making a collaborative map. Using large sheets of paper will mean three or four children can work on the drawing at the same time. Collaborative drawing provides a focus for the children's story talk.

● Review the story and ask the children to identify the places that Hannah visits. Note that the story starts and ends at home.

● Ask the children to make a map of the places that Hannah visits. Remind them to include her

home. The story provides no clues as to where the settings are in relation to each other, so the children can place them freely. Make sure all the children are involved in the drawing.

● Show the children how they can annotate the map to give information about what happens in each place. For example, at the zoo, *Hannah saw orang-utans, gorillas and chimpanzees.* At the cinema, *Hannah saw the film* Supergorilla.

● When the maps are finished, use them to support a retelling of the story.

Differentiation
For older/more confident learners: Challenge the children to make up a few extra settings for the story.
For younger/less confident learners: Support children for whom English is an additional language to annotate their map.

Just a dream?

Objective: To plan and write a story based on the themes from a known story.
What you need: Copies of *Gorilla*, stories about transformation (such as *The Snowman* by Raymond Briggs, *Where the Wild Things Are* by Maurice Sendak, *The Emperor of Absurdia* by Chris Riddell, *Kate the Cat and the Moon* by David Almond), photocopiable page 30.

What to do

● Ask pairs of children to read one of the stories and compare it with *Gorilla*. Ask: *What are the similarities/differences?* Note how each story has a magical transformation.

● Use an enlarged version of the photocopiable sheet to map the different stages in *Gorilla*: introduction to Hannah (opening); Hannah tries to get her father's attention (build up); Hannah is given a toy gorilla not a real one (problem),

Hannah and the gorilla have a night-time adventure (transformation), Hannah's father offers to take her to the zoo (resolution), they walk away hand in hand (ending).

● Let the children use the photocopiable sheet to plan their own stories based on a transformation. Suggest different ways to use the planner: as a frame to discuss ideas with a partner; making rough sketches for different stages of the story; making brief notes to give a suggestion of what happens.

● Ask the children to write their stories, before sharing and evaluating them as class.

Differentiation
For older/more confident learners: Challenge the children to be less formulaic with their planning.
For younger/less confident learners: Let the children analyse and retell a known story.

Get writing

Dear diary

● Re-read *Gorilla*. Think about how Hannah might be feeling throughout the story. Write her diary entries for Monday, Tuesday and Wednesday.

Monday	Dear diary, Dad was miserable this morning.
Tuesday	Dear diary, Something really amazing happened this evening.
Wednesday	Dear diary, This morning, when I woke up, I remembered that it was my birthday.

Gorillas

● Anthony Browne likes gorillas because they can be strong and gentle at the same time. Think about what you would like to find out about gorillas and write your questions in the concept map below.

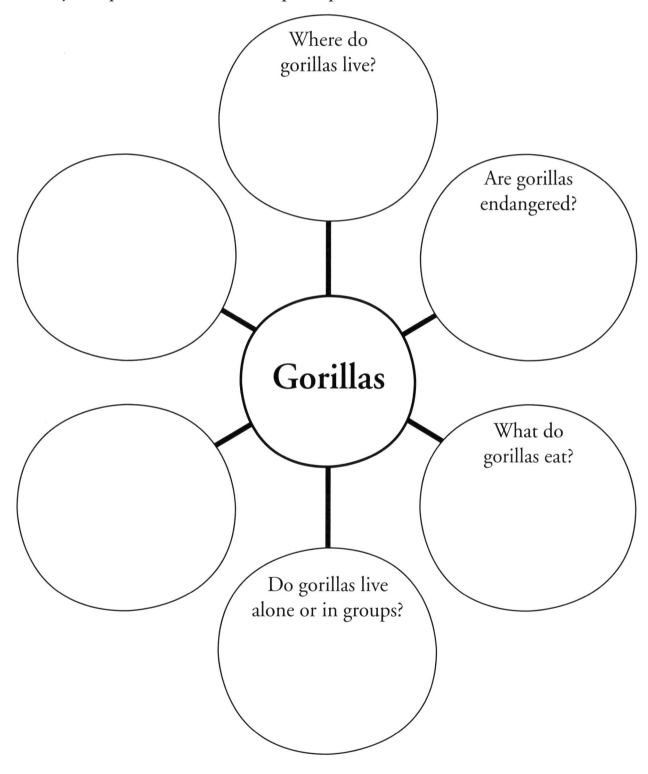

Just a dream?

● Use this story planner to plan your own story based on a transformation.

Opening	
Characters	
Setting	
Build up	
Problem	
Development (transformation scene)	
Resolution	
Ending	

Assessment

Assessment advice

The activities in this *Read & Respond* title provide opportunities for ongoing assessment of speaking and listening, reading and writing. In the guided reading sessions children are assessed on their ability to predict, infer and deduce. The activities require children to read the pictures, providing opportunities to assess visual literacy.

Various activities allow you to assess the children's engagement with the text through drama and other creative responses. An understanding of the book's main themes is elicited through dialogue and discussion.

Specifically, there is discussion about being alone and the ethics of keeping animals in zoos. Children should be encouraged to reflect on their learning by using reflective prompts, such as: *How did the drama aid our understanding of the characters in this story? What do I need to do next in order to improve my writing?*

The final assessment task allows for a review of what the children have learned about the central character, Hannah, as well as the themes of the book, through the creation of a personal page for a social networking website.

Hannah's page

Objective: To use evidence from a text to support ideas about character, theme and point of view.
What you need: photocopiable page 32, copies of *Gorilla*.

What to do
● Briefly discuss the children's knowledge of social networking websites, such as Beebo and Facebook. Show them some examples. Ask: *Does anyone keep a personal page? What sorts of things do you add to that page?*
● Distribute copies of the photocopiable sheet and explain to the children that they are going to create a personal page for Hannah, using evidence from the text to create the page.
● Talk through the photocopiable sheet together. Explain the 'what are you thinking' box (where they write what Hannah is feeling at the time), the wall posts (completed for different days of the week, indicating what Hannah is feeling at different times), and my five favourite things (the sorts of things Hannah would like). Some of these might be obvious because we are told about them in the story. However, others might be less obvious because they will have to think about the kind of character Hannah is and then decide what she might like. Hannah's favourite things might include toys, places, people and activities. List these as an *aide memoire* that the children can refer to when they are creating their pages.
● Once completed, organise the children in groups so that you can build in an opportunity for oral assessment. Invite them to talk about the page they have created and probe their reasons for identifying the five favourite things for Hannah.

Assessment

Hannah's page

● Re-read *Gorilla* and think about what Hannah is like and how she feels throughout the story. Create a social-networking profile page for Hannah, filling in the sections below.

	What are you thinking?
I am reading:	Wall post 3
I am watching:	Wall post 2
I am listening to:	Wall post 1

My top five favourite things: